Contents

Hunting hounds

The Kennel Club's Hound group is made up of 37 dog breeds. Most dogs in the Hound group were developed to work as hunting dogs. Scent hounds help hunters by locating prey with their noses. These dogs have a highly developed sense of smell that is even more sensitive than that of other dog breeds. Sighthounds, also called gazehounds, rely on their sharp eyesight and wide range of vision to locate prey.

Hounds vary in their personalities as much as they do in their appearances. Some are too loud to keep in flats or with close-by neighbours. Many hounds bark or howl frequently. Many are extremely athletic, while some are couch potatoes. Some are even both active and lazy – depending on the time of day. Some make excellent pets. Others prefer to spend their time in the field.

Whether they are working dogs or companions, hounds almost always have a desire to hunt. For this reason, fenced gardens and leads are important for keeping them safe. Although these dogs share the urge to hunt, they all have something special to offer dog lovers. Get ready for an up-close look at each Hound breed!

EDGE BOOKS™

Foxhounds, Greyhounds and Other

HOUND DOGS

by Tammy Gagne

Raintree is an imprint of Capstone Global Library Limited, a company incorporated in England and Wales having its registered office at 264 Banbury Road, Oxford, OX2 7DY – Registered company number: 6695582

www.raintree.co.uk
myorders@raintree.co.uk

Edited by Alesha Halvorson
Designed by Terri Poburka
Picture research by Kelly Garvin
Production by Katy LaVigne

ISBN 978 1 4747 2085 4 (hardback)
20 19 18 17 16
10 9 8 7 6 5 4 3 2 1

ISBN 978 1 4747 2099 1 (paperback)
21 20 19 18 17
10 9 8 7 6 5 4 3 2 1

British Library Cataloguing in Publication Data
A full catalogue record for this book is available from the British Library.

Acknowledgements
Newscom: Dorling Kindersley/Universal Images Group, 18 (bottom), 22 (b); Shutterstock: ARTSILENSE, 6 (b), Capture Light, 14 (top), cyanoclub, 28 (b), 8 (b), Dora Zett, 10 (b), DragoNika, 6 (t), 10 (t), 21 (t), 26 (t), Eric Isselee, 16 (b), 21 (b), 25 (b), Erik Lam, 12 (b), gbarinov, backcover, 11 (b), Grisha Bruev, 13 (t), Igor Normann, cover (top right), 4-5, Irina oxilixo Danilova, 15, Jagodka, 13 (b), 17 (b), 19 (b), 27, Lenkadan, 1, 12(t), 23 (t), Nick Hayes, cover (bottom right), Paul Cotney, cover (left), Pelevinia Ksinia, 24 (b), Rita Kochmarjova, 9 (t), Robynrg, 29, Rowena, 25 (t), saasemen, 17 (t), Sally Wallis, 20 (t), siloto, 11 (t), Steve Lovegrove, 16 (t), Svetlana Valoueva, 8 (t), Tatiana Katsai, 24 (t), terekhov Igor, 18 (t), tsik, 19 (t), Vivienstock, 7 (b), 28 (t), volofin 7 (t), WilleeCole Photography, 23 (b), www.BillionPhoto, 9 (b); Superstock: Jean-Michel Labat/ardea.com/Panth/Pantheon, 20 (b), John Daniels/ardea.com/Panth/Pantheon, 22 (t)

Printed and bound in the United Kingdom.

FUN FACT

The Kennel Club organizes many initiatives to aid dog owners in caring for their dogs. The Kennel Club runs Petlog, which is the UK's largest database for microchipped pets, in order to reunite lost dogs with their owners.

Afghan Hound

Appearance:

Height: 68 to 74 centimetres (27 to 29 inches)
Weight: 23 to 27 kilograms (50 to 60 pounds)

With its large body and long, silky hair, the Afghan Hound is an elegant breed. These dogs have long, narrow heads that help when hunting. They can see things both in front of them and far to each side.

Personality: Afghans are athletic dogs that love their human families. Fenced gardens are a smart idea for this breed because they are sighthounds. An Afghan won't just notice a squirrel – it will chase it down.

Breed Background: One of the oldest dog breeds, the Afghan Hound was developed to hunt gazelle, deer and even leopards.

Countries of Origin: Afghanistan, Iran, Pakistan

Training Notes: While Afghan Hounds are smart, they are also sensitive. They respond well to patience and lots of praise.

Care Notes: Afghans need a lot of exercise. They love to run in a large, contained area or be taken on daily walks. These dogs need their long coats brushed and washed daily.

FUN FACT

An Afghan Hound can run up to 64 kilometres (40 miles) per hour!

FAMOUS DOGS

Pablo Picasso created a 15-metre (50-foot) sculpture based on one of his Afghan Hounds. The piece stands at Chicago's Daley Plaza in the USA.

Basenji

Appearance:

Height: 40 to 43 centimetres (16 to 17 inches)
Weight: 9 to 1 kilograms (20 to 24 pounds)

This short-haired breed has several features that make it easy to recognize. First, people usually notice the dog's tightly curled tail. The breed also has a wrinkled forehead and large, pointed ears.

Personality: The Basenji's voice box is shaped differently than that of other breeds. For this reason Basenjis can't bark like other dogs. Instead they make a crowing-yodelling sound.

Breed Background: The Basenji was and is still used to hunt lions in Africa.

Area of Origin: Congo Basin

Training Notes: These intelligent dogs are extremely independent, so training takes time and effort. Early **obedience** training is important for Basenjis. **Socialization** at a young age is also a good idea.

Care Notes: Basenjis are known for getting into trouble when the opportunity arises. Owners who leave their belongings out may find them chewed up. Keeping a Basenji busy with plenty of exercise may help with his chewing habits. These dogs also need occasional bathing and brushing to keep them looking their best.

FUN FACT

Some hounds hunt with their noses. Others rely on their eyes. The Basenji uses both sight and scent in the field.

Basset Fauve De Bretagne

Appearance:

Height: 32 to 38 centimetres (13 to 15 inches)
Weight: 11 to 16 kilograms (25 to 35 pounds)

The Basset Fauve De Bretagne's reddish coat is wiry in texture. His legs are slightly shorter than the length of his back, but the Basset Fauve De Bretagne does not sit as low to the ground as the Basset Hound.

Personality: A Basset Fauve De Bretagne is lively, sweet and devoted. He makes a suitable pet for a small home and garden. This dog is also friendly with children.

FUN FACT

The Basset Fauve De Bretagne is sometimes called the **Fawn** Brittany Basset.

Breed Background: It is believed that this breed came from crossing a Griffon Fauve De Bretagne, a breed that is now extinct, and a Brittany Basset. The breed worked with flocks of sheep in the fields of France.

Country of Origin: France

Training Notes: The Basset Fauve De Bretagne needs firm and consistent training. He is also known for performing tricks for food!

Care Notes: The Basset Fauve De Bretagne loves to exercise! Because of this dog's short coat, grooming is an easy chore. He should be brushed and bathed occasionally to keep him looking his best.

Basset Hound

Appearance:

Height: 33 to 38 centimetres (13 to 15 inches)
Weight: 20 to 29 kilograms (45 to 65 pounds)

The Basset Hound has a heavy body, short legs and the longest ears of any dog breed. Many people think this breed has a sad expression because of the animal's droopy eyes but nothing could be further from the truth.

Personality: Bassets are affectionate and loyal dogs. They especially love spending time with children. Kids must be taught to treat these dogs with respect, however. Playing too rough with this breed can injure its long back.

Breed Background: Basset Hounds were developed by breeding Bloodhounds down to a smaller size.

Countries of Origin:

France, United Kingdom

Training Notes: Basset Hounds are stubborn dogs but easy to train. These dogs have a strong urge to hunt prey, especially hares, so training should begin at the puppy stage.

Care Notes: Because Basset Hounds are more likely to become **obese** than other breeds, daily exercise, including walks, is necessary. Weekly grooming, such as brushing the coat, is recommended. Owners must also clean their Basset Hounds' long ears frequently to prevent infection.

FUN FACT

Breeders who developed the Basset Hound chose dogs with white on their tails. The bright tip helped hunters spot the dogs even if they were in high brush.

Bavarian Mountain Hound

FUN FACT

The Bavarian Mountain Hound hails from Bavaria, Germany, where he is known as the *Bayerische Gebirgsschweisshund*.

Appearance:

Height: 44 to 52 centimetres (18 to 21 inches)
Weight: 18 to 25 kilograms (40 to 55 pounds)

The Bavarian Mountain Hound has a short, shiny coat, usually characterised by a darker face, head and ears. His coat is deer red, tan or fawn with interspersed black hairs. This pattern is called brindle.

Personality: There aren't many dogs more loyal than a Bavarian Mountain Hound. He makes a good family dog and is friendly with children. He can be **aloof** with strangers, however.

Breed Background: The Bavarian Mountain Hound was bred to be a hunting dog in Germany's mountainous regions. He specialises in tracking large wounded game, such as wild boar and deer. The Bavarian Mountain Hound can follow game over huge distances many hours after the game's trail has been left.

Country of Origin: Germany

Training Notes: The Bavarian Mountain Hound is responsive to a respectful owner. He easily learns commands and obedience with positive reinforcement, such as treats or praise.

Care Notes: The Bavarian Mountain Hound needs a considerable amount of exercise each day. His nose may lead him to trouble or danger, so walking without a lead is not recommended.

Beagle

Appearance:

Height: 33 to 40 centimetres (13 to 16 inches)
Weight: 9 to 11 kilograms (20 to 25 pounds)

Beagles can be almost any colour, except all white. By far the most popular variety is the **tricolour**. This combination is made up of a black **saddle**, tan head and middle and white everywhere else.

Personality: Beagles are one of the most popular hounds, both as a family companion and in the show ring. They are friendly with their owners and most strangers. Beagles have a loud bark, however.

Country of Origin: United Kingdom

Training Notes: Beagles are smart dogs. Non-hunting Beagles must be kept on leads or in fenced yards outdoors, however. These determined animals will follow any scent that tempts them. Because of their independent personality, short training sessions may work best with Beagles.

Care Notes: Beagles are playful and need a fair amount of exercise each day. Despite their short coats, Beagles need frequent baths. If anything smelly is nearby, this breed will surely roll in it. Weekly brushing is also important for these shedders.

FUN FACT

Beagles have a special sound they make when hunting. They use it to let the hunter know they are following the scent of their prey.

FAMOUS DOGS

The famous *Peanuts* cartoon character Snoopy is a Beagle.

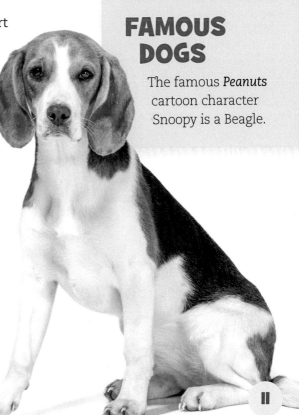

Bloodhound

Appearance:
Height: 61 to 66 centimetres (24 to 26 inches)
Weight: 36 to 41 kilograms (80 to 90 pounds)

Bloodhounds have sturdy bodies, long ears and lots of wrinkles. The breed's short, thin coat comes in several colours. Black and tan or red are common coat colours for this dog.

Personality: A Bloodhound can make a wonderful pet. People considering buying this breed should know how much Bloodhounds drool – a lot!

Breed Background: Some people think that the Bloodhound got its name from its ability to smell blood. Bloodhounds have the most powerful noses of any dog breed. They actually got their name from their pure bloodlines.

Countries of Origin: Belgium, England, France, Scotland

Training Notes: Owners can train Bloodhounds to do almost anything – except not follow their noses. Obedience training should begin during the puppy stage for these dogs.

Care Notes: Bloodhounds need lots of daily exercise to prevent boredom. These dogs should be brushed and bathed weekly to help them look and smell their best.

Borzoi

Appearance:

Height: 68 to 74 centimetres (27 to 29 inches)
Weight: 27 to 48 kilograms (60 to 105 pounds)

Borzois are large but graceful dogs. Their long, silky coats can be flat, curly or wavy. Any colour is acceptable for this breed.

Personality: The Borzoi is known for its incredible speed and endurance. As active as they are, these dogs love spending time with their owners. Dog enthusiasts say the Borzoi is among the most loving and gentle dog breeds.

Breed Background:

The Borzoi was developed by crossing Arabian Greyhounds with sheepdogs.

Country of Origin: Russia

Training Notes: Borzois need extra time and patience when training. They are naturally stubborn. Using praise and rewards, such as treats, may help a Borzoi warm up to obedience training.

Care Notes: Similar to other sighthounds, the Borzoi cannot be trusted off his lead in public. A high, fenced garden is ideal for daily running and exercise. This breed's long coat should be brushed regularly to keep it shiny and **mat**-free.

FUN FACT

The Borzoi is also known as the Russian Wolfhound. The word borzii is Russian for "swift".

Dachshund

FUN FACT

Some people call Dachshunds hot dogs because of their length. But the food was actually named after the animal. Hot dogs were called "dachshund sausages" when they were first created.

Appearance:

Standard
Height: 20 to 27 centimetres (8 to 11 inches)
Weight: 9 to 12 kilograms (20 to 26 pounds)

Miniature
Height: 13 to 18 centimetres (5 to 7 inches)
Weight: less than 5 kilograms (11 pounds)

Dachshunds are long dogs that stand low to the ground. Their coats can be smooth-haired, wire-haired or long-haired. These dogs come in two sizes – standard or miniature. Both are members of the same breed. The most common Dachshund colours are black and tan, red and Silver Dapple.

Personality: The Dachshund is a popular pet that bonds closely with his owners. The breed is an excellent house-dog and will guard against any unwelcome guests. His bark can be surprsingly deep for a small dog.

Breed Background: The Dachshund breed can be traced back to working dogs in Germany. These dogs could get low enough to the ground to hunt game such as badgers and rabbits.

Country of Origin: Germany

Training Notes: This breed is smart but stubborn. Owners may spend a lot of time training a Dachshund, especially with housetraining. Patience and **persistence** are recommended with this breed. Dachshunds respond well to positive rewards, such as praise or treats.

Care Notes: Dachshunds love to dig. For this reason owners must supervise their pets whenever they spend time outside. To avoid becoming overweight, Dachshunds should exercise regularly. Weekly brushing or combing is important for all coat types of this breed.

Deerhound

Appearance:

Height: 71 to 76 centimetres (28 to 30 inches)
Weight: 37 to 46 kilograms (80 to 100 pounds)

The Deerhound's coat is thick and shaggy. Most Deerhounds are dark blue-grey, although the breed comes in a variety of other colours too. Some are sandy-red, shades of yellow or red fawn.

Personality: This friendly, athletic dog can make a great family pet as long as he gets his exercise. The only thing a Deerhound enjoys more than going for a long walk is resting afterwards.

FUN FACT

Deerhounds are so easygoing that they cannot be trained to be watchdogs. Being **aggressive** just isn't in their nature.

Country of Origin: Scotland

Training Notes: This breed can be difficult to train. Deerhounds delight in their owners' praise, but they prefer doing what they like. Early socialization and obedience training may help with this issue.

Care Notes: Exercise is very important for Deerhounds. They need space to run on a daily basis. Deerhounds are shedders. Their coats need brushing about twice per week to remove dead hair.

Finnish Spitz

Appearance:

Height: 39 to 50 centimetres (16 to 20 inches)
Weight: 14 to 16 kilograms (31 to 35 pounds)

The Finnish Spitz looks a bit like a fox. His square body is covered with a thick double coat. Males usually have fuller coats than females. All dogs are a golden-red colour and can range from a pale honey to a deep red-brown.

Personality: Developed as hunting dogs, Finnish Spitzes remain highly active. Many still hunt in their native country. They can also make excellent pets for families because they get along well with children. Intensely loyal, a Finnish Spitz will protect his human family when necessary.

Country of Origin: Finland

Training Notes: The Finnish Spitz is a smart dog but bores easily. To keep this breed focused, train often but only for short periods of time. These dogs respond well to positive praise and rewards.

Care Notes: A Finnish Spitz needs a lot of exercise each day. A rigorous play session in a fenced area can help use up this dog's energy. Because it is a heavy shedder, regular brushing and bathing is important.

FUN FACT

The Finnish Spitz is the national dog of Finland.

Foxhound

Appearance:
Height: 58 to 64 centimetres (23 to 25 inches)
Weight: 29 to 32 kilograms (65 to 70 pounds)

The Foxhound has a short, tricoloured coat. The hair is black, white and tan and has a rough texture. This hard texture protects the dog from both harsh weather and low branches.

Personality: Foxhounds are friendly, gentle dogs. Despite their loving nature, they're not usually kept as pets. These dogs are meant for people who will take them hunting often. They are happiest when working as part of a pack of Foxhounds in the field.

Breed Background: The Foxhound is one of the few dog breeds that continues to be bred for its original purpose – hunting.

Country of Origin: United Kingdom

Training Notes: As pack animals, these dogs learn many hunting techniques from watching their fellow Foxhounds. Training Foxhounds requires patience and understanding. They respond well to loving but firm leadership.

Care Notes: Daily exercise is ideal for this breed. A Foxhound's short coat should be brushed regularly to keep it looking shiny.

FUN FACT
Foxhounds are bred to run for kilometres at a time.

Greyhound

Appearance:
Height: 69 to 76 centimetres (27 to 30 inches)
Weight: 27 to 36 kilograms (60 to 80 pounds)

The Greyhound looks like he was built for speed. His thin body and long legs make him the fastest dog in the Kennel Club. This sighthound also has a long, thin head that gives him a wide field of vision. He can see what is behind him without turning his head.

Personality: Greyhounds make ideal pets for active families. Despite their large size, these loving animals think they are lapdogs. Greyhounds are highly affectionate, faithful and gentle.

Country of Origin: Unknown; believed to be Egypt

Training Notes: Greyhounds are easy to train but require patience. Early obedience training works well with Greyhounds.

Care Notes: Because of their tendency to run, Greyhounds need daily exercise in a large, fenced area. Their short coats do not require much grooming except occasional brushing and bathing.

FUN FACT

Greyhounds can reach speeds over 70 kilometres (45 miles) per hour after running just 15 metres (50 feet)!

FAMOUS DOGS

Harry Potter author J.K. Rowling adopted her Greyhound, Sapphire, from an animal shelter.

Ibizan Hound

Appearance:

Height: 56 to 74 centimetres (22 to 29 inches)
Weight: 19 to 25 kilograms (42 to 55 pounds)

The Ibizan Hound has two coat types: short-haired or wire-haired. The breed also comes in three colours, including chestnut or lion solid colour, white or a combination of these. The dog's flesh-coloured nose and eye rims give the breed a unique look.

FUN FACT

The Ibizan Hound's nickname is the "Beezer".

Personality: Ibizan Hounds are affectionate and highly loyal to their human family members. These dogs take more time to warm up to strangers, however.

Country of Origin: Egypt

Training Notes: This breed learns quickly but becomes bored easily. Owners will have the best luck keeping training sessions short and fun. Early socialization training may also help Ibizan Hounds with warming up to new people.

Care Notes: Fenced yards give Ibizan Hounds the space to move that this breed needs. It is important that the fence is at least 1.8 metres (6 feet) high. An Ibizan Hound can jump anything shorter. Its rough, short coat requires only occasional brushing and bathing.

Irish Wolfhound

Appearance:
Height: 71 to 79 centimetres (28 to 31 inches)
Weight: 41 to 55 kilograms (90 to 120 pounds)

The Irish Wolfhound is the tallest of all dog breeds. Many people joke that this dog looks more like a horse than a dog. Horses definitely do not have this breed's rough and wiry coat, however. After his size, the breed is best known for his shaggy coat.

FUN FACT

An Irish Wolfhound can measure up to 2 metres (7 feet) tall when standing on his hind legs.

Personality: This huge breed needs plenty of space to run and play. An Irish Wolfhound is great with children, but he should be supervised around small children because of his size.

Breed Background: The Irish Wolfhound is one of the oldest dogs still living today. It dates back to AD 391. The breed was developed to hunt elk, wild boars and wolves.

Country of Origin: Ireland

Training Notes: It is essential to begin training this breed when it is a puppy. Handling an **unruly** adult Irish Wolfhound is a challenging task for most people. If properly trained, Irish Wolfhounds will excel at dog sports in the show ring.

Care Notes: New owners of this breed should be prepared to buy lots of dog food. An adult Irish Wolfhound can eat 11 kilograms (25 pounds) of food in just one week. Despite its size an Irish Wolfhound doesn't need much exercise. Weekly brushing is important for these shaggy dogs.

Otterhound

Appearance:
Height: 61 to 69 centimetres (24 to 27 inches)
Weight: 30 to 52 kilograms (66 to 115 pounds)

The Otterhound's coat is dense and harsh, and his hair always looks messy. The thick double coat comes in many different colours and combinations. The most common combination is black and tan.

Personality: Otterhounds are loving pets. They are best suited for active families. Owners should take this dog along when going to the beach or lake whenever possible. Otterhounds greatly enjoy swimming and being in the water.

Countries of Origin: United Kingdom, France

Training Notes: Otterhound owners should make early socialization a top priority. Training may require patience, persistence and positive rewards and praise.

Care Notes: This breed needs plenty of space for regular exercise. Weekly brushing is important to keep an Otterhound's hair clean and tangle-free.

FUN FACT

The Otterhound is considered one of the most endangered dog breeds worldwide. It is rarer than the Giant Panda.

Pharaoh Hound

Appearance:

Height: 53 to 63 centimetres (21 to 25 inches)
Weight: 20 to 25 kilograms (45 to 55 pounds)

The Pharaoh Hound's short coat, muscular body and pointed ears make this breed easy to spot anywhere. His coat can be tan or rich tan with white markings on his chest, face, tail and toes.

Personality: Pharaoh Hounds love their human family members and are entertaining. These dogs aren't as friendly with new people, however. When a stranger arrives, a Pharaoh Hound can become aloof.

Breed Background: The Pharaoh Hound looks a lot like dogs in Ancient Egyptian art. This is no accident, as the breed dates back to 1,000 BC in this part of the world.

Country of Origin: Egypt

Training Notes: Pharaoh Hounds are highly intelligent and enjoy pleasing their owners. The breed can be stubborn, so training is important early on.

Care Notes: This breed feels cold easily. Dogs living in cooler climates should wear coats for time spent outdoors. These athletic dogs also need daily exercise. Their short coats need to be brushed every other week.

FUN FACT

The Pharoah Hound is the National Dog of Malta.

Rhodesian Ridgeback

Appearance:

Height: 61 to 69 centimetres (24 to 27 inches)

Weight: 29 to 41 kilograms (65 to 90 pounds)

The Rhodesian Ridgeback is a large, muscular dog with a short coat. The breed is easy to identify by the ridge on its back. This long line is created by fur that grows in the opposite direction from the other hair in this area. The breed was named for this unusual feature.

FUN FACT

A Rhodesian Ridgeback can keep pace with a running horse for up to 48 kilometres (30 miles).

Personality: Rhodesian Ridgebacks make great companions for families with older kids. Their high activity level makes them a perfect match for active people. This is a dog that wants to spend lots of time outdoors.

Breed Background: Also known as the African Lion Dog, this breed was developed to hunt large cats.

Area of Origin: Rhodesia (present-day Zimbabwe), southern Africa

Training Notes: This smart breed is highly independent. Patient and consistent training works best with Rhodesians.

Care Notes: Rhodesian Ridgebacks are very athletic and need at least an hour of exercise each day. Because they have short coats, Rhodesians shed very little and require only weekly brushing.

Saluki

Appearance:

Height: 58 to 71 centimetres (23 to 28 inches)
Weight: 14 to 25 kilograms (31 to 55 pounds)

The Saluki looks a lot like a long-haired Greyhound. He has a long, thin body that helps him move quickly. These dogs are lean but incredibly muscular. Their feathery coats come in a variety of colours, including white, cream, red, tricolour or black and tan.

Personality: Salukis can be shy and take their time warming up to people. These dogs are suited for active families who will take the time to challenge them both physically and mentally.

Breed Background: Royal Ancient Egyptians turned their Salukis into mummies when the dogs died.

Country of Origin: Egypt

Training Notes: The Saluki can be naughty if left alone. The Saluki's aloof nature can make training difficult. Patience and consistency are important, as well as early obedience training.

Care Notes: One of the best ways to provide this breed with the exercise it needs is to take it jogging. Salukis can keep up with even the most athletic human runners. These dogs don't shed a lot, but they should still be brushed weekly and bathed occasionally.

FUN FACT

The name Saluki is believed to have originated from the long-gone Arabian city of Saluk or from the town of Seleukia in ancient Syria.

Whippet

Appearance:

Height: 44 to 51 centimetres (18 to 20 inches)
Weight: 9 to 18 kilograms (20 to 40 pounds)

Whippets are medium-sized sighthounds with great speed and balance. These short-haired dogs come in a variety of colours and markings, including black, blue, cream, red and white. Whippets are a breed of muscularity and neatness paired with power and elegance.

Personality: Named for their whip-like speed, these dogs are surprisingly calm when they're not playing. They enjoy napping on the floor or sofa. Some dogs will even snuggle with their favourite human family member.

Country of Origin: England

Training Notes: Whippets are smart but sensitive. They need positive, gentle training. They respond well to praise and other rewards.

Care Notes: These athletic dogs excel at canine sports, such as **agility**. Without an organized activity, Whippets need a large amount of daily exercise. Their short coats should also be brushed weekly and bathed occasionally.

FUN FACT

In the northeast of England, some racing Whippets have been known to cover over 180 metres (200 yards) in as little as 12 seconds!

Basset Griffon Vendeen (Petit) ▶

Appearance:
  Height: 34 to 38 centimetres (14 to 15 inches)
  Weight: 11 to 16 kilograms (25 to 35 pounds)
Known for: its nickname – the PBGV
Country of Origin: France

. . . .

Cirneco Dell'Etna ▼

Appearance:
  Height: 42 to 52 centimetres (17 to 20 inches)
  Weight: 10 to 12 kilograms (22 to 26 pounds)
Known for: ability to hunt
  by sight and sound
Country of Origin: Italy

. . . .

Harrier ▶

Appearance:
  Height: 48 to 50 centimetres
  (19 to 21 inches)
  Weight: 18 to 27 kilograms
  (40 to 60 pounds)
Known for: being talented
  hunters and friendly pets
Country of Origin: United Kingdom

....

Norwegian Elkhound

Appearance:
  Height: 49 to 52 centimetres (20 to 21 inches)
  Weight: 20 to 23 kilograms (44 to 51 pounds)
Known for: loud voice
Country of Origin: Norway

....

Portuguese Podengo

Appearance:
  Height: 20 to 30 centimetres (8 to 12 inches)
  Weight: 4 to 5 kilograms (9 to 11 pounds)
Known for: National Breed of Portugal
Country of Origin: Portgual

....

Glossary

aggressive strong and forceful

agility ability to move fast and easily

aloof distant or not friendly

fawn light brown colour

mat thick, tangled mass of hair

obedience obeying rules and commands

obese very fat

persistent continually trying to do something

poacher person who hunts illegally

saddle coloured marking on the back of an animal

socialize train to get along with people and other dogs

tricolour having three colours

unruly hard to control or discipline

Read more

Caring for Dogs and Puppies (Battersea Dogs & Cats Home Pet Care Guides), Ben Hubbard (Franklin Watts, 2015)

Everything Dogs (National Geographic for Kids), Becky Baines (National Geographic, 2012)

Looking After Dogs and Puppies (Pet Guides), Katharine Starke (Usborne Publishing Ltd, 2013)

Websites

http://animals.nationalgeographic.com/animals/mammals/ domestic-dog/
Learn all about domestic dogs through photos, videos, facts and more on this National Geographic website.

www.ykc.org.uk/
Become a member of the Young Kennel Club and discover lots of different events you and your dog can attend, including training and fun agility days.

Index